D0745599

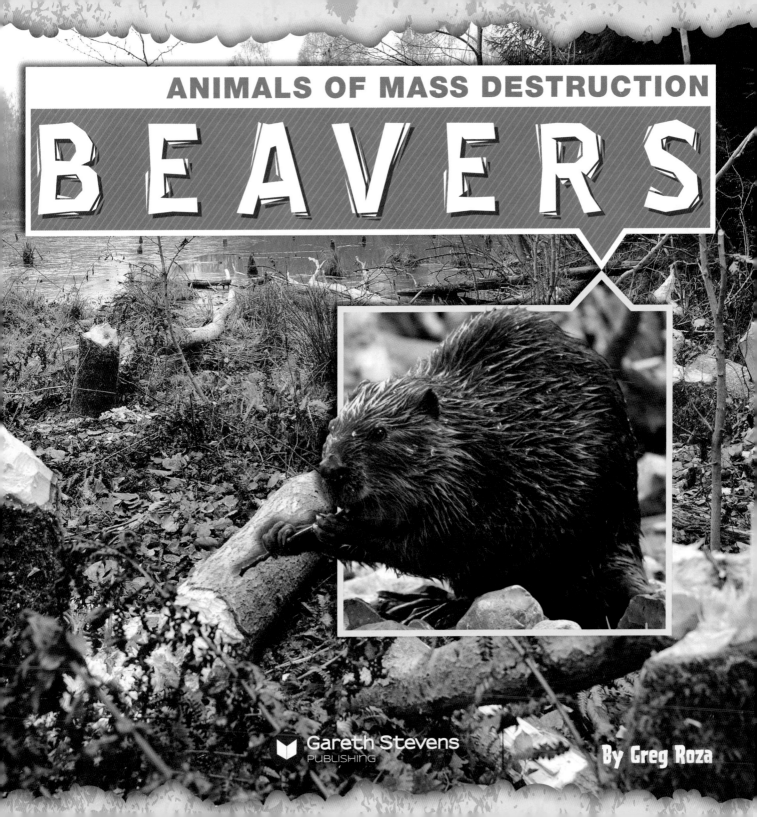

ANIMALS OF MASS DESTRUCTION

BEAVERS

Gareth Stevens
PUBLISHING

By Greg Roza

Please visit our website, www.garethstevens.com. For a free color catalog of all our high-quality books, call toll free 1-800-542-2595 or fax 1-877-542-2596.

Library of Congress Cataloging-in-Publication Data

Roza, Greg.
Beavers / by Greg Roza.
    p. cm. — (Animals of mass destruction)
Includes index.
ISBN 978-1-4824-0797-6 (pbk.)
ISBN 978-1-4824-1023-5 (6-pack)
ISBN 978-1-4824-0796-9 (library binding)
1. Beavers — Juvenile literature. I. Roza, Greg. II. Title.
QL737.R632 R69 2015
599.37—d23

First Edition

Published in 2015 by
Gareth Stevens Publishing
111 East 14th Street, Suite 349
New York, NY 10003

Copyright © 2015 Gareth Stevens Publishing

Designer: Andrea Davison-Bartolotta
Editor: Therese Shea

Photo credits: Cover, p. 1 (main) KOO/Shutterstock.com; cover, p. 1 (inset) Alan Jeffery/Shutterstock.com; series art (all textured backgrounds, yellow striped line) Elisanth/Shutterstock.com; series art (caption boxes) Fatseyeva/Shutterstock.com; series art (purple boxes) Tracie Andrews/Shutterstock.com; pp. 4–5 Pictureguy/Shutterstock.com; pp. 6–7 Berthier Emmanuel/hemis.fr/Getty Images; p. 7 (map) cobalt88/Shutterstock.com; p. 7 (footprints) PhotoHouse/Shutterstock.com; p. 8 Stephen J. Krasemann/Photographer's Choice/Getty Images; pp. 8–9 Universal Images Group via Getty Images; p. 10 © iStockphoto.com/Andyworks; pp. 10–11 belizar/Shutterstock.com; pp. 12–13 Brad Thompson/Shutterstock.com; p. 14 Tyler Olson/Thinkstock; pp. 14–15 UbjsP/Shutterstock.com; p. 16 Pi-Lens/Shutterstock.com; pp. 16–17 Photopictures/Shutterstock.com; pp. 18–19 Dorling Kindersley/Vetta/Getty Images; p. 20 Karl-Joseph Hildenbrand/AFP/Getty Images; pp. 20–21 Ken Hoehn/Thinkstock; p. 22 Joel Sartore/National Geographic/Getty Images; pp. 22–23 Henrik Larsson/Shutterstock.com; p. 24 Helen H. Richardson/The Denver Post via Getty Images; pp. 24–25 Steve Russell/Toronto Star via Getty Images; p. 26 ekler/Shutterstock.com; pp. 26–27 Johnathan Esper/Shutterstock.com; p. 28 Little_Things/Thinkstock; pp. 28–29 MyLoupe/Universal Images Group via Getty Images.

Printed in the United States of America

CPSIA compliance information: Batch #CS15GS: For further information contact Gareth Stevens, New York, New York at 1-800-542-2595.

CONTENTS

Words in the glossary appear in **bold** type the first time they are used in the text.

BUSY BEAVERS

Have you ever seen beavers building a dam? If so, then you're sure to understand the phrase "busy as a beaver." Beavers are well known for gnawing down trees with their strong teeth. They use the trees to build dams and homes called lodges.

Beavers' hardworking nature helps the **environment** in some ways. However, their activities can also be very **destructive**. Their dams can drive some animals from their homes. Beaver dams can cause flooding or stop water from reaching farms. Beavers can wipe out whole forests!

Chew On This!

Beavers are mostly nocturnal. That means they're busy at night and sleep during the day.

Beavers like to eat the inner layer of bark on some kinds of trees. They eat leaves and twigs, too. They often use the rest of the "debarked" tree for dams and lodges.

WHERE TO FIND THEM

There are two **species** of beavers. The North American beaver lives from Canada to Mexico and from the Pacific Ocean to the Atlantic Ocean. These beavers don't live in deserts or the far north, though. You may have seen North American beavers in a body of water near where you live.

The Eurasian beaver once lived all over Europe and Asia. Due to overhunting, it's now found in smaller numbers in France, Germany, Poland, **Scandinavia**, and Russia.

Chew On This!

North American beavers were introduced to Argentina and Scandinavia around 1940. The species grew quickly in both locations.

North American beaver

Eurasian beaver

both species

This map shows where the two kinds of beavers live.

Eurasian beaver

7

LOOK THE PART

Beavers are the second-largest **rodent** in the world and the largest rodent in North America. The largest beavers grow to be about 40 inches (102 cm) long and can weigh up to 70 pounds (32 kg). Like all rodents, beavers have special front teeth for gnawing.

Beavers are well known for their broad, flat tail, which can be up to 12 inches (30 cm) long. When a beaver senses danger, it warns other beavers by slapping the water with its tail. Beavers also groan when talking to each other.

beaver tail

Chew On This!

Beavers have body parts that make weird-smelling oil called castor. They use it to mark their territory. People use castor to make perfume, medicines, and even some foods.

A beaver's tail is nearly furless. It's covered with black scales.

TOUGH TEETH

Everyone knows beavers have some of the strongest teeth around. These include two upper front teeth and two lower front teeth called incisors, which never stop growing. Beavers use these long, curved teeth to gnaw wood and tear open food. The teeth are **chisel** shaped, which helps cut through tough plants. Gnawing wears down the teeth and keeps them from growing too long.

What makes a beaver's teeth so strong? They have **iron** in their hard outer covering. It also makes them orange!

Chew On This!

Beavers have very strong jaw muscles. Strong teeth and powerful jaws allow beavers to gnaw through even large trees in little time—especially when they're working together.

The iron in a beaver's teeth comes from the trees they eat, such as cottonwood, willow, maple, aspen, and others. They also eat aquatic plants, such as water lilies.

READY FOR THE WATER

Beavers are semiaquatic—they spend part of their time on land and part in water. They love slow-moving bodies of freshwater. Their large, webbed back feet are perfect for swimming, and their tail helps them turn quickly underwater. When they're underwater, special lids protect their eyes, and flaps close their ears.

Beavers have two layers of fur, which helps keep them warm in cold water. They use their castor to waterproof their fur. Beavers also have a thick layer of fat to keep them warm.

Chew On This!

Even underwater, beavers can gnaw on wood. Their front teeth stick out past their lips, so they can still keep their mouth closed to keep water out.

Beavers swim under the ice in winter!

KITS AND COLONIES

Between April and July every year, female beavers give birth to up to nine babies, called kits. Kits can swim within 24 hours. Both mother and father help care for the young. In fact, beaver couples often stay together for life and raise many kits together.

Beaver families live in groups called colonies. Young beavers stay with their parents for 2 years. Then, the parents send the young beavers away to start their own colonies.

Chew On This!

Colonies create dams that change the environment and may force other animals to move away.

Beavers can live for about 20 years. During that time, they eat a lot of trees!

WOOD AND WATER

Beavers need freshwater and wood to live. They can live in many kinds of **biomes**, including forests, lakes, streams, mountains, and wetlands. Some even make their homes in ditches in towns and cities. When there isn't enough water for them, they build dams to create pools.

Beavers spend much of their time collecting wood to build dams and lodges or searching for food. Often, they do both at the same time. They use a lot of wood!

Chew On This!

Beavers dig **burrows** in the mud near a body of water.

beaver lodge

Beavers cut down trees so they can nibble away at their bark and use the rest for construction projects. But they leave the trees they don't like, such as elms.

AT HOME WITH BEAVERS

Many beaver lodges are cone-shaped homes made of wood, rocks, and grass. Some can be 20 feet (6 m) wide at the base and 10 feet (3 m) high. Beavers seal their lodges with mud, but they may leave openings in the top to let fresh air in.

Chew On This!

Beavers often store sticks underwater in case they need food during the winter.

Lodges may have several underwater entrances. This keeps colonies safe from enemies. Beaver predators include wolves, coyotes, foxes, otters, bears, and some large birds. Unfortunately, beaver homes can cause big problems for others.

Inside the Lodge

1. food supply
2. living area
3. underwater entrances
4. lodge
5. raised water
6. dam

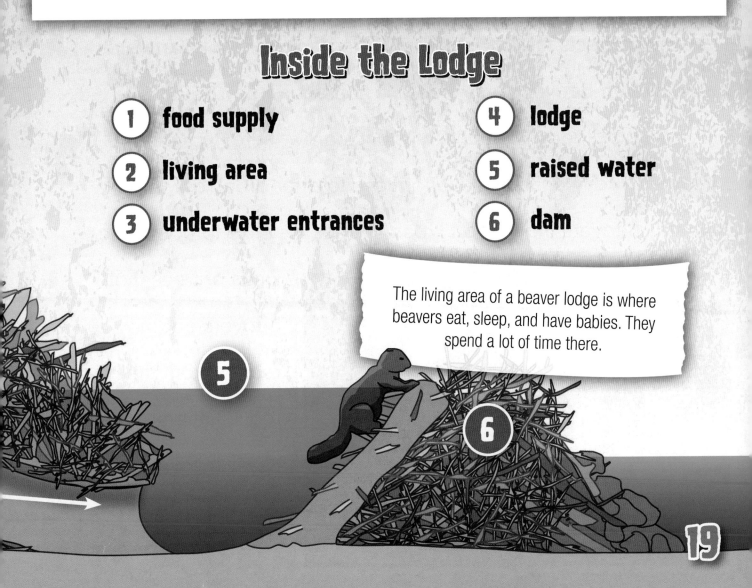

The living area of a beaver lodge is where beavers eat, sleep, and have babies. They spend a lot of time there.

BIG CHANGES

Few wild animals can change their environment as much as beavers can. Dams change small creeks into large ponds, which affects the types of plants and animals that live there. Although beaver dams create a home for many aquatic animals, floods kill plants that once grew there, including trees. Many animals have to move to drier areas as well.

Beavers may kill off types of trees they like to eat. Some kinds of trees that beavers eat may regrow from their roots. Others never recover.

While beavers are destructive to some tree species, they help other trees grow and spread—the ones they don't like to eat!

BAD BEAVER!

Beavers can be a major problem for farmers. Dams flood farmland and damage valuable crops and timber. They also flood roads and other public areas.

The ponds created by beaver dams attract bugs that can be pests to people. Beavers may gnaw on your favorite trees in your backyard!

Beavers can spread a few illnesses to people through drinking water, too. These illnesses cause bad stomachaches, fever, throwing up, and other problems. However, other animals are known to spread these illnesses, too, not just beavers.

Beavers like to create large ponds so they don't have to travel far on land to reach food. They have to worry about more predators on land.

Chew On This!

One of the illnesses that beavers spread is sometimes called "beaver fever." It's caused by creatures so tiny you can't see them without a microscope.

CITY BEAVERS

Early fur trappers in North America killed so many beavers they almost became **extinct**. However, beavers have returned to many of North America's rivers, streams, and lakes. In some cases, beavers have settled close to and in cities.

Natural locations near cities can be the hardest hit by beavers. Golf courses and parks lose trees. But some beavers travel further along streams and rivers into a city itself. It's hard and costly to trap and remove beavers from a city.

Chew On This!

In spring 2013, a beaver colony settled along the Guadalupe River in downtown San Jose, California. These were the first beavers in the area in over 150 years!

beaver trap

Over the years, beavers have grown used to people. But don't get too close—they bite.

TAKING OVER

In the 1940s, 50 North American beavers were set free in the forests of Tierra del Fuego, Argentina. The government had hoped to start a fur industry. Unfortunately, they found out that North American beavers are an **invasive** species in that environment.

Today, there are more than 100,000 beavers on Tierra del Fuego. There are no natural predators to control them. The trees there don't grow back like many trees in North America. In some places, beavers have turned whole forests into treeless **bogs**.

Tierra del Fuego, Argentina

South America

Argentina

In order to save the forests of Argentina, scientists have decided the beavers need to be hunted and removed.

LIVING TOGETHER

People have long been beavers' greatest predator. Since laws slowed beaver trapping for fur and castor, beaver numbers have grown again. Now some people are wondering if beavers should be hunted more to reduce their sometimes destructive habits.

Today, there are special **devices** that help stop or control flooding due to beaver dams. There are fences that go around trees to keep the beavers from eating them. Solutions like these and others may help people and beavers live peacefully together in the future.

baby beavers

Most experts agree that beavers are usually more helpful than they are harmful.

beaver antiflooding device

GLOSSARY

biome: a natural community of plants and animals, such as a forest or desert

bog: an area with wet ground, mostly made up of plant matter that's breaking down

burrow: a hole made by an animal in which it lives or hides

chisel: a metal tool with a straight, flat end used for cutting and shaping wood or stone

destructive: causing a lot of damage

device: a tool or machine made to perform a task

environment: the natural world in which a plant or animal lives

extinct: no longer living

invasive: likely to spread and be harmful when placed in a new area

iron: a strong, hard, silvery-gray metal

rodent: a small, furry animal with large front teeth, such as a mouse or rat

Scandinavia: Denmark, Norway, Sweden, and sometimes Iceland, the Faroe Islands, and Finland

species: a group of plants or animals that are all the same kind

FOR MORE INFORMATION

Books

George, Lynn. *Beavers: Dam Builders*. New York, NY: PowerKids Press, 2011.

Gibbons, Gail. *Beavers*. New York, NY: Holiday House, 2013.

Websites

About Beavers
www.beaversww.org/beavers-and-wetlands/about-beavers/
Learn more about North American and Eurasian beavers.

History of the Fur Trade
www.montanatrappers.org/history.htm
Read about the history of the North American fur trade.

What to Do About Beavers
www.humanesociety.org/animals/beavers/tips/solving_problems_beaver.html
Find out how people are working to protect both beavers and people's property.

INDEX